Make Waves

A Career Pathing Guide to Stand Out, Stay Employed, and Sail Ahead

Theresa Hummel-Krallinger

Theresa Hummel-Krallinger
theresa@highfiveperformance.com
www.highfiveperformance.com

BRIGHT
WAKE
PRESS

Published by Bright Wake Press
Book design by Hedy Sirico

Make Waves, Theresa Hummel-Krallinger —1st ed.

ISBN: 0991321405
ISBN-13: 978-0991321407

Testimonials

"*Make Waves* by Theresa Hummel-Krallinger provides invaluable, proven processes and insights for navigating your job search — before, during and after accepting a new position.

Theresa has built sterling credentials and expertise as a creative corporate trainer/educator, humorist, entrepreneur and networker. Her passion, inspiration, and motivational talents as a consummate speaker and storyteller are woven into this book.

As one of the founders of My Career Transitions, and leader in many other organizations, Theresa has been a guiding light for hundreds of job seekers, even for me, as her former career transition consultant. From the moment I met Theresa, I knew she had embraced the journey and was in control of her career choices and decisions.

Make Waves provides lifeboats against the challenging swells in the tempest of the work world. "Make Waves" should be on the top of your bookshelf, consulted throughout your professional travels across an ever-shifting world of work. I am certain it will become a must read, lifelong career-management resource for anyone seeking or contemplating a change in employment."

STAN GUY
Retired Managing Director, MidAtlantic District, DBM

"In most "self-help" books, you get a lot of advice, but you are left to figure out how to implement it yourself. "Make Waves" is the rare book that not only tells you the best ways to conduct a job search, but it gives you the tools you need to do it. From the opening chapter, Theresa Hummel-Krallinger, relates to the reader by describing her own experience being laid off and looking for a job. She interjects humor with her clear, direct, and compassionate understanding of the job search experience. Then, through the tools and exercises she provides throughout the book, it's as if she is sitting next to you and walking you through the process that will lead to a successful job search. As a Career Coach, I highly recommend this book to anyone looking for a new opportunity or just looking to manage their career more effectively."

KEN SHER
Executive Coach

"There's no one better suited to help you navigate your path in the professional world than Theresa Hummel-Krallinger! What might seem like an overwhelming challenge is broken down into clear, actionable steps that anyone can follow. With her expert guidance, Theresa helps you find your way to the career you not only want but truly deserve. Her writing is both simple and powerful, and as you read, you can almost see your own journey taking shape, your boat slowly coming together. Theresa encourages you to reflect honestly on where you are, what you excel at, and where you have room to grow—always with a gentle, caring approach that is one of her signature qualities. For me, this book was a reminder of how Theresa helped me chart my own course and start making waves in my career. If you're looking to find your direction, I wholeheartedly recommend following these steps. I can personally attest to their effectiveness! Thank you, Theresa, for sharing your wisdom and helping all of us build careers that are both fulfilling and meaningful."

ROB DELANEY
People Manager, Mentee, Fan

"In *Make Waves: A Career Pathing Guide to Stand Out, Stay Employable, and Sail Ahead*, Theresa Hummel-Krallinger offers a step-by-step plan for navigating every stage of your career — from your first job through to retirement, including that ever-elusive work-life balance. Theresa equips readers with practical tools like checklists, resource lists, QR codes, and real-world examples to help you not just start strong, but stay on course.

I wish I'd had this book — and Theresa's powerful sailboat model — when I was launching my career, and again when I started my own business. The way she breaks down how career pathing works, how to build a success-focused plan, and how to actually work that plan is both pragmatic and empowering. It would've saved me from more than a few missteps.

Whether you're just starting out or charting a new course, this guide is the smart, steady hand you need to navigate your career with purpose."

ANNMARIE KELLY
Bestselling Author, The Five-Year Marriage, Victorious Woman!

"Practical. Powerful. Personal. Theresa Hummel-Krallinger has created the ultimate career guide for anyone who wants to stop drifting and start driving their career boat with confidence. *Make Waves* will help you stand out, stay employable, and sail ahead. This is your career insurance policy for the future of work."

DAVID NEWMAN
Author of Do It! Marketing *and* Do It! Selling

Dedication

Many thanks to those who showed me the ropes when I needed it most, those early years when I jumped out on my own, especially Stan Guy and Ford Myers – two of the best career consultants I know. Also, Deanne Bryce, Franne McNeal, and Annmarie Kelly – smart businesswomen who were also very supportive as I went out on my own.

And

To my family, husband Rik, sister Brigid, and "sister" Cindy who have always encouraged and supported me.

And

To my supporters that have passed on, especially Mom and Dad, brother Charlie, sister Kitty, Aunt Peg, Charmaine Hummel, Liz McShea, Ellen Shea, Geri Beyer, Mary Lou Ling, Debra Lynn Ambrose, Rose Quinn and cousin Bernice.

Table of Contents

Introduction

PAIN DRIVES CHANGE.

In the spring of 1996, I was working in the corporate training department for a systems organization within a large insurance company. I remember coming to work that day and seeing our VP looking out the window of our building onto the campus, lost in thought. I said a quick hello and made my way to my desk. Our group of approximately 150 professionals in the business systems department was scheduled to attend a major meeting at 10 a.m. in our Education Center.

At about 9:30, a helicopter landed on the helipad. This was a rare sighting. We occasionally had senior leaders arrive by helicopter, but it was an unnecessary extravagance. Our corporate headquarters was about 90 minutes up the PA / NJ Turnpike, so most executive commutes were by car. On this day, however, they wanted a quick in and out. We would soon find out why.

At 10 a.m., we shuffled downstairs to the big meeting. We grabbed cold beverages and light snacks, then took our seats. Our local VP opened the presentation by introducing his boss and the corporate VP of HR. She showed us the first slide and said, "As a leadership team, we are always looking for ways to help the organization run efficiently." Then she breezed through a couple of slides showing the current org charts for the systems organization. "Based on our research, we found work at this location is redundant."

REDUNDANT

The word echoed off the walls of the room and through my head. It was as if she were speaking in slow motion. She advanced to a slide with an org chart that showed staff in NJ, MN, and FL. Hmmm. Where did PA go? Perhaps we have our own special slide. Right?

No special slide for PA. The rest of the presentation was a blur. The room was so silent, it was as if we weren't even breathing. Time stood still. The HR VP took over the presentation and said, "You will all be instructed on how your work will be transitioned. Some will be done in 30 days, some in 60 days, some in 90 days. To assist us, we've enlisted the support of Lee Hecht Harrison, an outplacement firm. At 11 a.m., you will meet in smaller groups with an outplacement consultant to discuss next steps."

How did this happen? One day, I was a valuable employee. Today, I am redundant.

The meeting concluded before 10:30, leaving us about a half-hour to spare before we met with the outplacement team. Our VP sheepishly escaped the room with the two senior VPs. Within minutes, the two VPs from NJ were whisked by car to the helipad, where they quickly escaped to the corporate office.

I wandered the all-too-familiar halls for about 20 minutes, trying to make sense of what had just happened.

Twelve years, damn it. Twelve good years I gave them. I was a good employee. I worked hard. I showed up. I did what I was told. What sense does this make? How can they toss us out like yesterday's trash? They don't even know us. We grew up here. Most of us joined the company right out of school, be it high school or college. We celebrated each other's engagements, weddings, births, and anniversaries. We supported each other through deaths, divorces, and other emotional challenges. We vacationed together. We played together. We were family. This isn't just the loss of a job; it's the loss of our community.

Now what? Where will I go? I don't even have a resume. I don't even know where to begin. I've never felt more vulnerable.

And then, I had an epiphany: I realized that I didn't ever want to feel this way again. I realized that I must OWN my career. I can no longer be at the whim of my employer. I must, at any given time, be ready to jump. From this point forward, **I will pilot my career boat!**

I went from feeling desperately hopeless to fully empowered. It's incredible what a decision will do for you!

And so it began … my love for … my obsession with … my lifelong commitment to career management. I have been at this, full-steam ahead, since 1996. This mindset shift has created employment insurance for me. It has changed my life for the better. And it will, should you choose to accept this mission, change your life as well.

PAIN DRIVES CHANGE. OWNING YOUR CAREER CHANGES EVERYTHING.

"Out of suffering have emerged the strongest souls; the most massive characters are seared with scars."

Khalil Gibran

DIRECTION | EXPERIENCE | CREDIBILITY | KNOW PEOPLE

SECTION 1:
Anchors Aweigh!:
An Introduction to the "Career Boat"

IN THIS SECTION, WE'LL COVER:

• Why this matters by sharing data & trends in the job market.

• Building your career boat to get you on DECK: Direction, Experience, Credibility and Knowing People

• Assessing your current career boat

WHY THIS MATTERS

"A ship is safe in harbor, but that's not what ships are for."

John A. Shedd

Time at work is a large percentage of our waking hours in our lifetime. Most people have some form of employment from age 18 through their late 60s. Assuming we take a full-time job by at least age 21, retire at age 67, and have an average of three weeks of vacation each year, that's 10,856 days we spend at work.

Through the 1980s, many people who landed a job with a secure organization often stayed with that company their entire career. When I first joined that large insurance company in the mid-'80s, there were many employees with 20, 30, and 40 years of service. While there are still organizations with large populations of tenured employees, that is certainly not the norm anymore.

ACCORDING TO THE U.S. BUREAU OF LABOR STATISTICS, INDIVIDUALS BORN BETWEEN 1957 AND 1964 HELD AN AVERAGE OF 12 JOBS FROM AGES 18 TO 54, WITH THE MAJORITY OF CHANGES OCCURRING BEFORE AGE 40.

(Source: U.S. Bureau of Labor Statistics, National Longitudinal Survey, 2021)

Other projections, including those shared by Forrester Research, suggest that today's youngest workers may hold as many as 12 to 15 jobs over their lifetimes as career paths continue to evolve.

This underscores just how fast the career landscape is shifting, reminding us that managing your career is no longer a once-in-a-while activity — it's an ongoing practice.

IN A 2017 REPORT, THE INSTITUTE FOR THE FUTURE PROJECTED THAT 85% OF JOBS IN 2030 HADN'T EVEN BEEN INVENTED YET – A PREDICTION THAT FEELS EVEN MORE REAL AS WE APPROACH THAT MILESTONE.

(Source: Institute for the Future & Dell Technologies, The Next Era of Human-Machine Partnerships, *2017.)*

This means most people are not fully equipped for the demands of today's workplace — creating both a challenge and a tremendous opportunity for those willing to continuously learn and adapt.

ACCORDING TO THE U.S. BUREAU OF LABOR STATISTICS, ABOUT 32% OF WAGE AND SALARY WORKERS IN 2022 HAD BEEN WITH THEIR CURRENT EMPLOYER FOR LESS THAN TWO YEARS, HIGHLIGHTING THE INCREASING FLUIDITY OF MODERN CAREER PATHS.

(Source: U.S. Bureau of Labor Statistics, Employee Tenure Summary, September 2022)

If you are a security-based person, this information may be unsettling. If, however, you embrace change, this is the working world for you!

Either way, it is critical that we have a strong career management plan for your entire working life. That's right. You will need this plan for your whole working life. If you already have a plan, you're ahead of the pack. If not, this book will show you how to create one.

Having worked with jobseekers since 2003, the importance of this content has been drilled into my head. I watch year after year as job seekers of all ages flock to job-search groups. Some of them are in their 40s, 50s, and 60s, and it may be their first job search in decades. Long gone are the days when all you needed was a resume and a newspaper to find a job.

These older job seekers are starting from scratch and are overwhelmed. The emphasis on networking, online resources like LinkedIn, and a demand for technology-savvy candidates can be daunting for someone who has been comfortably employed for the last couple decades, especially if they haven't kept their skill set up to date.

However, this book is for everyone in the workforce:

• Fresh graduates looking for a way to build a foundation for their lifelong career plan

• Older professionals who find themselves in an unexpected job search

• Any person who wants to feel a sense of control over their employment situation by staying relevant, skilled, and well-networked.

Building Your Boat

In 2003, not long after I had gone through my second downsizing, I began delivering a presentation to jobseekers called, "Are you Bobbing Along or Making a Wake?: Career Management Skills for Turbulent Times." Back then, unemployment was high. We were still reeling from the aftermath of 9/11a few years prior. There was a need for conversation not only about how to stay afloat, but also how to make progress during tough times.

In a career support group that I started through our local ASTD (American Society for Training and Development) chapter (now they are ATD, Association for Talent Development). I delivered that program for about a dozen or so jobseekers. (That's where this whole boat analogy started.) **I have now delivered that presentation to hundreds of jobseekers for over 20 years.**

Essentially, your career boat comprises 4 parts:

D = Direction. Your career goal is the rudder of your ship.

E = Experience. Your skills and knowledge are the body of your boat.

C = Credibility. Your credentials are your sails.

K = Know People. Your professional network is your motor.

Each element is important to your career success. Some parts are more important than others, depending on what your career goal is.

DIRECTION:
YOUR CAREER GOAL IS THE RUDDER

Not all boats have rudders, right? For instance, a raft has no rudder. If you're on a raft in a strong current, you'll go where the waters take you. Where you'll end up can't be predicted or prepared for. You just hold on for the ride and hope for the best.

That was me early in my career. I completely trusted that my company would take me to a good place. Yet, that is not the job of the company. The job of the company is to run a good business. Yes, it's wise for an organization to train and take care of its employees to a certain extent. Ultimately, though, it's the employee's responsibility to own his/her career.

Without a goal, it's hard to plan for and maintain a career plan

If you don't have one, you're not alone. I've met people of all ages that haven't figured out what they want to be when they grow up.

In Chapter 2, we'll spend time exploring the tools that will help you determine a career goal. Among them are several assessments: Myers Briggs (personality); Interest Inventory; Values; Strengths; and DISC (behavior style.)

If you are lucky enough to already have a career goal, you can probably skip Chapter 2.

EXPERIENCE:
SKILLS AND KNOWLEDGE ARE THE BODY OF YOUR BOAT

The body of your boat (your skills and knowledge) is extremely important. In fact, if you only focus on one thing, building skills and knowledge would be it. In order to find work, you need to be able to add value. And, you do that by contributing something worthwhile, which usually requires specific skills and knowledge.

Some things are easy to learn, like, making a pair of earrings. I can teach you how to do that in under one hour, and you'll be fairly proficient.

Other things take time, like being a project manager. Sure, you can read a book. Take some classes. Ultimately, though, serving as a project manager is the true test of how qualified

"Before the journey begins, a sailor must ensure the ship is seaworthy."

Anonymous

you are to successfully manage a project. To prove your ability at adding value and be hired as a project manager, it's a good idea to have some educational qualifications (perhaps a certification), a track record of successfully completed projects you've led, and some testimonials from folks who've worked with you on projects.

In a future chapter, we'll discuss ways you can build and reinforce the body of your boat, which is your job skills and experience.

CREDIBILITY:
YOUR JOB CREDENTIALS AND REPUTATION ARE THE SAILS

Not all boats have sails, but those that do are able to use the winds to propel them across the water. In our boat analogy, the sails represent your credentials and professional reputation.

For many jobs, it's helpful to have a third party validate that you've completed an educational program that prepares you for work. That program might be a college degree, be it an associate's, bachelor's, master's, or doctoral. It might also be a certification program, where you are tested at the end, and are sometimes required to continue education to maintain that certification. You might also obtain credentials through certificate programs or workshops that focus on a specific skill or set of skills.

You'll often see required credentials in job descriptions. This is to ensure that only qualified, credentialed applicants apply. However, these requirements can also eliminate qualified candidates who have acquired their skills and knowledge through experience or apprenticeship, rather than through an educational program.

Along with credentials, your reputation—often referred to as "personal brand"—is very important. You build your personal brand through your professional accomplishments, as attested to by your colleagues and customers, or by being seen as a thought leader through writing articles and books, or speaking on that topic.

Another important factor that impacts personal brand is how you treat other people.

CREDIBILITY + LIKABILITY = PERSONAL BRAND

It's important to know what credentials are often required for a specific job or job family, as well as how personal branding plays into ensuring you are a credible job candidate. We'll talk more about this in a future chapter.

KNOW PEOPLE:
YOUR PROFESSIONAL NETWORK IS THE MOTOR

When the job market is good, it's as if strong winds are blowing that will help carry the boat along by using the sails. The motor (professional network) becomes less important, though it is always helpful. When the job market is not good, the winds have stopped, and even the best credentials in the world won't help you without the motor.

As a former leadership mentor, Jean Otte used to say, "It's not who you know. It's who knows you know." She could not be more right! In times of job transition, a strong professional network is the power we need to find and land a new job.

Sadly, many people don't focus on building and maintaining a professional network while they're still gainfully employed. This is a mistake.

We'll spend some time learning how to jumpstart, build, and maintain a strong professional network throughout your career in a future chapter.

Draw Your Boat

BASED ON WHERE YOU ARE NOW IN YOUR CAREER, DRAW A PICTURE OF YOUR BOAT. DON'T WORRY ABOUT BEING PERFECT! THIS IS JUST TO GET YOU THINKING ABOUT THOSE AREAS OF YOUR BOAT THAT NEED ATTENTION.

WHAT PARTS OF YOUR BOAT NEED THE MOST ATTENTION?

_____

_____

_____

_____

SECTION 2:
Finding Your Rudder:
Defining Your Career Goal

IN THIS SECTION, WE'LL COVER WAYS TO DETERMINE YOUR BEST CAREER GOALS BY ASSESSING YOURSELF. WE'LL DISCUSS SEVERAL EXERCISES THAT WILL HELP YOU DETERMINE YOUR INTERESTS, MARKETABLE SKILLS, YOUR PERSONALITY, VALUES, STRENGTHS AND PERSONAL MISSION.

WHY THIS MATTERS

Alice asks,"Would you tell me, please, which way I ought to go from here?"

The Cheshire Cat responds, "That depends a good deal on where you want to get to."

Alice then asks, "I don't much care where."

The Cat concludes, "Then it doesn't matter which way you go."

Lewis Carroll, Alice's Adventures in Wonderland

Finding Your Rudder – Career Direction

An important part of the career management process is having a career goal upon which to focus. I must admit, for the first part of my career, I was a bit of a raft. I really had no rudder. Sure, at college I thought I had a goal. Yet, once I was out in the working world, I just needed to make money and take a job, any job. I really didn't have a career goal until I fell into the corporate training department at that large insurer.

The universe has this way of steering you toward the things you're meant to do. I have always had a knack for teaching and training. Even when I took the interest inventory in high school, the number two job suggested for me was personnel administrator. (For those who may not know, "Personnel" was the precursor to "Human Resources" and corporate training is a subset of Human Resources.)

Falling into corporate training was a blessing. For that season of my life, that is exactly where I was meant to be. And I was doubly blessed to do it at that insurance company, where I learned from the best of the best.

No matter what season of life you are in, it's never too late to find your rudder! I have met people of all ages, including those in their 60s, who are unsure of what they want to be when they grow up. If you'd like a little help figuring this out, there are several assessments and exercises that will help you.

Intersection of the Circles – Finding Your Sweet Spot

I first came across The Hedgehog Concept in Jim Collins' bestseller, "Good to Great." He found that the greatest companies operated from their sweet spot. Those that didn't might be good, but they'd never be considered great.

So, what is the sweet spot? It's the intersection of three circles:

1. What do you enjoy doing?
2. What are you naturally good at?
3. What will people pay you for?

If you can find the intersection of those circles, that is your sweet spot.

Later on, I found an expanded model from Japan called Ikigai (pronounced EEKEE GUY). In this model, a fourth circle is added that asks, "What does the world need?"

The meaning of Ikigai is, "A reason for being". So beautiful!

TAKE SOME TIME TO EXPLORE THIS MODEL FOR YOURSELF.

What is your ikigai? Once you get some ideas down, it's fun to bounce ideas off some people who know you well. Ask them: "What am I naturally good at?"

Draw four intersecting circles below, as shown in the previous image. Label each intersection: Passion, Mission, Vocation, Profession.

1. PASSION + MISSION: WHAT DO YOU LOVE TO DO?

_____

2. PASSION + PROFESSION: WHAT ARE YOU NATURALLY GOOD AT?

_____

3. MISSION + VOCATION: WHAT DOES THE WORLD NEED?

_____

4. PROFESSION + VOCATION :WHAT WILL YOU BE PAID FOR?

_____

What's Your Personality?

My personality type is ENFP / INFP (I am right on the 50% line for introvert/extrovert.) A great resource that I've used for career choices is, "Do What You Are: Discover the Perfect Career for You Through the Secrets of Personality Type," by Paul and Barbara Tieger. It can be ordered online, or you will likely find a copy at your local bookstore.

In lieu of that book, do an internet search on "careers for ENFP" or whatever your 4-letter type is. You will, no doubt, find many resources with suggestions for you.

According to most personality type theories and thought leaders, a person's type is inherent and does not change. However, individuals can develop behaviors, traits and habits that differ or even directly contradict the description of their type. We'll look at another assessment to focus on behavior called DISC.

Since personality does not change (or it doesn't change much), it is, therefore, a good anchor for researching career choices. It's a reflection of who you are and how you're wired. When you are in a career choice that is not in alignment with your personality, it is a very uncomfortable feeling, and usually not very fulfilling.

(I just did a quick search for careers for ENFP and felt validated. Career Counselor was one of the top items on the list. Boom!)

You can do a Google search to find a free Myers Briggs assessment. Here's a link and QR code to one I like: https://www.16personalities.com/free-personality-test

E EXTROVERTED	**S** SENSING	**T** THINKING	**J** JUDGING
I INTROVERTED	**N** INTUITIVE	**F** FEELING	**P** PERCEIVING

WHAT IS YOUR MYERS-BRIGGS TYPE?

____ ____ ____ ____

WHAT CAREERS ARE LISTED FOR YOUR MYERS-BRIGGS TYPE THAT STAND OUT AS POSSIBILITIES FOR YOU?

"If you say making money is the most important thing, you will spend your life completely wasting your time. You'll be doing things you don't like doing in order to go on living. That is, to go on doing things you don't like doing. Which is stupid. Better to have a short life, which is full of what you like doing, than a long one spent in a miserable way."

Alan Watts

Interest Inventory

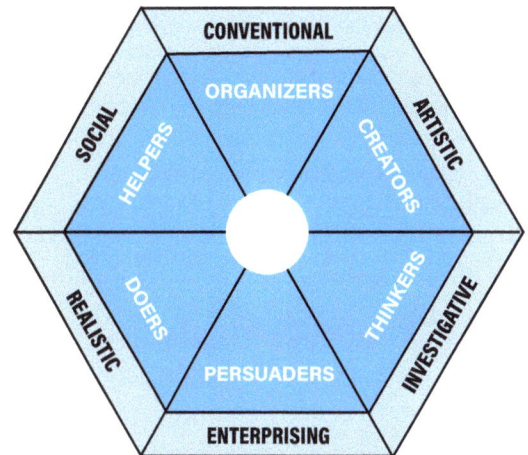

Another great tool to help you determine your career goal is the Interest Inventory. This tool helps you find a career that aligns with your interests. Several tools can help you, including the Strong Interest Inventory and the Holland Code, among others. The one I recommend is free of charge and can be completed online: O*NET.

Not only will O*NET point you to career choices that are a fit for your interests, it will also provide information on education requirements and job outlook. It's a wonderful tool!

Once you've completed your assessment, you'll receive a report with the top three scores of the General Occupational Themes:

- Realistic
- Investigative
- Artistic
- Social
- Enterprising
- Conventional

On my last assessment, my top three were SAE: Social / Artistic / Enterprising. A list of jobs that are a "best fit" and a "great fit" are shown in "job zones" by the amount of preparation needed. It's no surprise that several jobs that are part of my resume are on that list: career / business / communications teacher and counselor.

Here's a link and QR code to O*NET Online: https://www.onetonline.org/

WHAT ARE YOUR INTEREST INVENTORY RESULTS?

Realistic   _____

Investigative   _____

Artistic   _____

Social   _____

Enterprising   _____

Conventional   _____

YOUR JOB ZONE:

_____

WHAT ARE JOBS THAT CAME UP ON YOUR LIST THAT ARE GOOD POSSIBILITIES FOR YOU?

_____

_____

_____

What matters most to you?

Back in 2000, I had the privilege of participating in a women's leadership development program in New York City called Women Unlimited. Approximately 40 women in manager- and director-level positions came together once a month for a year.

As part of that curriculum, we did an exercise where we each received a deck of 50 value cards. We were asked to spread out the entire deck so we could see all the values. Once the deck was splayed, we were asked to pinpoint our top 10 values. All the values were good, so it was tough to discard any. Little by little, we all narrowed our pile down to 10 values.

Then, the instructor said, "Now, narrow it down to five cards." Wow. This was challenging. After much consideration, each of us peeled away five cards. We were asked to prioritize those cards from highest to lowest in importance, and set those five cards to the side.

With the cards aside, we were asked to look at the number of hours in a week. There are 168 hours in a week. In your typical work week, divvy up how you spend your time. If you're lucky, you get the recommended 8 hours of sleep each night. So, allot 56 hours (or whatever is typical for you) for sleep. Allot time for anything that falls into your typical weekly routine: self-care (showers, dental care, etc.), exercise, chores, time with family/friends, commute time, time at work and/or doing work-related tasks, meals, hobby time, non-work-related meetings.

Once you have accounted for all 168 hours, bring back your five value cards. As best you can, align values with the times on your time list. For example, if one of your values is "family," how much time do you spend with family? If "health" is one of your top five values, how much time do you spend ensuring good health? This exercise can be quite eye-opening.

I remember one of the women in our program was brought to tears. She cried because so little of her time was spent on the five values that she had identified. She talked about coming home from work late in the evening, giving a half-hearted greeting to her significant other and her pet, grabbing a quick bite to eat, and getting back to work before going to bed.

Many of the women in that group were career-driven, so we could relate. Yet, for some, that aligned with their values. If they had selected "Career Achievement" or "Financially Secure," the workaholic lifestyle might be in alignment with their values.

You'll find a values assessment in the Addendum, and also by visiting the following QR code.

"Focus on making choices to lead a life that aligns with your core values in the most purposeful way possible."

Roy T. Bennett

WHAT ARE YOUR TOP THREE TO FIVE VALUES?

1. _____

2. _____

3. _____

4. _____

5. _____

HOW DO YOU SPEND YOUR TIME EACH WEEK (168 HOURS)?

HOW MUCH TIME DO YOU SPEND ON YOUR TOP VALUES?

VALUE 1

_____

▪ Hours/Minutes:

VALUE 2

_____

▪ Hours/Minutes:

VALUE 3

_____

▪ Hours/Minutes:

VALUE 4

_____

▪ Hours/Minutes:

VALUE 5

_____

▪ Hours/Minutes:

TOTAL TIME EACH WEEK SPENT ON YOUR TOP VALUES?

What are you naturally good at?

I was first introduced to the strengths assessment through work done by the Gallup Organization. Back then, thought leaders Marcus Buckingham and Curt Coffman published a book with an online assessment, "Now Discover Your Strengths." It has since been updated by Tom Rath as "Strengthsfinder 2.0."

Inside the book is a code that allows you to take the assessment online. You can also purchase the assessment without the book. Once completed, you will receive a comprehensive report listing your top five of 34 strengths.

Here's a link and QR code to this assessment:
https://www.gallupstrengthscenter.com/

If you choose to complete that assessment, please make a note of your top 5 strengths. Consider how much time you spend using your top 5 strengths.

YOUR TOP FIVE STRENGTHS:

1. _____

2. _____

3. _____

4. _____

5. _____

HOW MUCH TIME DO YOU SPEND ON YOUR TOP FIVE STRENGTHS?

STRENGTH 1
_____
· Hours/Minutes:

STRENGTH 2
_____
· Hours/Minutes:

STRENGTH 3
_____
· Hours/Minutes:

STRENGTH 4
_____
· Hours/Minutes:

STRENGTH 5
_____
· Hours/Minutes:

TOTAL TIME EACH WEEK SPENT ON YOUR TOP STRENGTHS?

> ## "The strength of the ship lies not in the size of its sails, but in the quality of its build."
>
> *Anonymous*

How do you respond to the environment?

My favorite self-assessment of all is DISC because it feels like a personality assessment, but it's really measuring how you respond to the environment.

Like Myers-Briggs, there are online and paper DISC assessments and 4-style assessments like DISC. Many companies sell these assessments. I work with a great company in Minnesota, and am happy to provide you with access to a report for a small fee.

Essentially, there are four primary styles:

D – Dominance
I – Influencer
S – Supportive
C – Conscientious

Each of us is a blend of the four styles, with one usually being a primary behavioral driver.

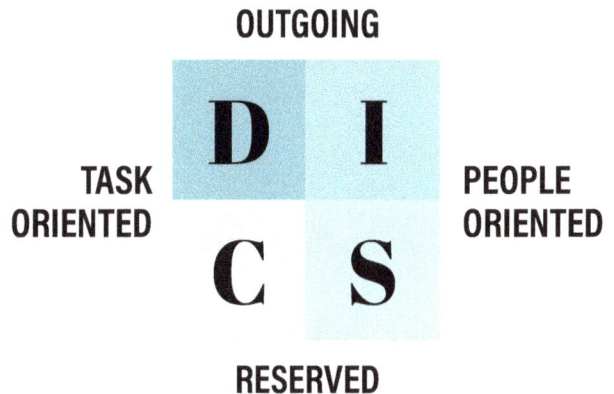

OUTGOING

TASK ORIENTED

D I

C S

PEOPLE ORIENTED

RESERVED

D

THE DOMINANCE STYLE is outgoing and task-oriented. These folks are movers and shakers, and like to get things done. They tend to percolate up to leadership roles, regardless of their title. They prefer to work in a challenging, fast-paced work environment.

I

THE INFLUENCER STYLE is outgoing and people-oriented. The "I" style is energetic and enthusiastic, and sees life as full of possibilities. They are often excellent communicators. They are idea-generators and like to work in a flexible, fun work environment.

S

THE SUPPORTIVE STYLE is reserved and people-oriented. The "S" style is the consummate team player. They are service-oriented, dependable, and helpful. They value peace and cooperation. They enjoy a collaborative, steady work environment.

C

THE CONSCIENTIOUS STYLE is reserved and task-oriented. They are perfectionistic and value factual information and doing things "right." Their research and analytical skills are valuable to teams and organizations. They prefer to work in a businesslike atmosphere where quality is valued.

Once you have your primary DISC style, it is a helpful indicator of not only jobs that are a fit for you but also the kind of work environment in which you'll do best.

Over the years, my DISC style has evolved from "SI" to "ISD." Your DISC style can evolve over time, influenced by your experiences and environment.

Here's a free DISC assessment: https://www.tonyrobbins.com/disc/

"To chart a course, first know thyself; for no sailor can navigate without understanding their own ship."

Anonymous

WHAT IS YOUR PRIMARY DISC STYLE?

BASED ON THAT STYLE, WHAT DOES IT TELL YOU ABOUT YOURSELF IN TERMS OF:

STRENGTHS:

AREAS FOR DEVELOPMENT:

ALIGNMENT WITH CERTAIN JOBS:

THE TYPE OF JOB ENVIRONMENT THAT IS CONDUCIVE FOR YOU TO DO YOUR BEST WORK:

KNOW PEOPLE | CREDIBILITY | **EXPERIENCE** | DIRECTION

SECTION 3:
Strengthening the Hull:
Building Skills & Experience

IN THIS SECTION, WE'LL COVER WAYS TO BUILD THE SKILLS AND EXPERIENCE NEEDED TO ATTAIN THE TYPES OF JOBS YOU WANT.

• Assessing what you already have

• Ways to build skills and get experience before you have a job

• Creative ways to convey your experience

WHY THIS MATTERS

"Success doesn't come from what you do occasionally; it comes from what you do consistently."

Marie Forleo

Building Skills & Knowledge – Experience

So often we see job openings requiring at least two years or more experience. If you're a recent graduate or someone who has only a short amount of work experience, this will be an essential chapter for you.

Here's the good news: You already have skills and knowledge. There are some things you already know how to do and do well. Let's start there. Reflect on your career journey, including jobs, volunteer roles, education, hobbies, and personal projects. Let's do a personal SWOT analysis to gather some information.

If you've never done a SWOT analysis before, it's a great tool to help you determine:

• STRENGTHS
Personal strengths or characteristics that give you an advantage in achieving your goals. These can be skills, qualities, resources, or anything that sets you apart from others.

• WEAKNESSES
Personality traits, bad habits, or gaps in your skill set that may hinder your progress or pose challenges. Weaknesses are areas where you may need improvement or development.

• OPPORTUNITIES
External factors and situations that you can leverage to your advantage. Opportunities are things like market trends, job openings, personal connections, or any external factors that could help you achieve your personal goals.

• THREATS
Potential threats that could hinder your progress or pose a risk to your goals. Threats could include competition, economic downturns, personal obstacles, or anything else that might impede your success.

SAMPLE PERSONAL SWOT:

	STRENGTHS	WEAKNESSES
INTERNAL	Good communication skills Well-organized Customer service skills Good with MS Office products Problem solver	Easily stressed Slow learner Perfectionist Not assertive
	OPPORTUNITIES	**THREATS**
EXTERNAL	Previous employers Networking Customer recommendations Remote work	Those with stronger technology skills Rejection Limited local opportunities

"In times of change, the learners will inherit the earth, while the learned find themselves beautifully equipped for a world that no longer exists."

Eric Hoffer

NOW YOU TRY:

	STRENGTHS	WEAKNESSES
INTERNAL		

	OPPORTUNITIES	THREATS
EXTERNAL		

WHAT STRENGTHS CAN YOU BUILD ON AND USE MOST?

_____

WHAT CAN YOU DO TO WORK AROUND OR DIMINISH WEAKNESSES?

_____

WHAT CAN YOU DO TO TAKE ADVANTAGE OF THE OPPORTUNITIES?

_____

WHAT CAN YOU DO TO MITIGATE THREATS?

_____

Now take SWOT a step further. Meet with people who know you well and want you to succeed. Do the SWOT exercise with them to see if they come up with other information for each of the 4 categories.

	STRENGTHS	WEAKNESSES
INTERNAL		

	OPPORTUNITIES	THREATS
EXTERNAL		

WHAT DO THEY SEE AS STRENGTHS YOU CAN BUILD ON AND MOST USE?

WHAT IDEAS DO THEY HAVE FOR YOU TO WORK AROUND OR DIMINISH WEAKNESSES?

WHAT DO THEY SEE AS OPPORTUNITIES YOU CAN TAKE ADVANTAGE OF?

WHAT SUGGESTIONS DO THEY HAVE FOR MITIGATING THREATS?

KNOW PEOPLE | **CREDIBILITY** | EXPERIENCE | DIRECTION

SECTION 4:
Building Your Sails:
Enhancing Your Reputation & Credibility

IN THIS SECTION, WE'LL COVER WAYS TO BUILD THE REPUTATION AND CREDIBILITY NEEDED TO ATTAIN THE TYPES OF JOBS YOU WANT. WE'LL COVER PERSONAL BRANDING AND EDUCATION QUALIFICATIONS.

WHY THIS MATTERS

"It's not what you know. It's who knows you know."

Jean Otte, Founder, Women Unlimited

Now that you have a sense of direction with your rudder (career goal), and your hull (skills and knowledge), it's time to build some power for your boat. We build power through our sails (personal brand) and our motor (professional network). With tall sails and a powerful motor, we can easily navigate through our career, even during stormy weather or times when there is no wind.

As some of you know, life doesn't always go as planned. I once saw a baby bib with a delightful quote, "Spit happens." So true, right? We're moving along happily and then … dribble …. spit happens.

Some of us spend significant time gaining credentials, which are an important component of our sails. Yet, we fall off the wagon after college by not continuously learning and earning updated credentials. Others may do a good job of keeping up with their education, but fail to invest in the people and relationships in their network.

These are the keys to a successful career kingdom:

1) Be really good at what you do.

2) Make sure people who can help you know you're really good at what you do.

3) Be someone others want to work with.

Period.

Continuously hone your skills and knowledge through gaining work experience and formal education. Continuously build and maintain a strong professional network. Create experiences with others that make them want to work with you. This takes intentional effort. You will be doing this every day throughout your work life. This is the secret sauce for a successful career.

Would you like to learn how to do just that? Read and do the exercises in this section!

BUILDING YOUR PERSONAL BRAND

• What is your brand? What do you want it to be?

• Johari Window / Nohari Window

• 360 Feedback

• Branding opportunities

• Use of social media

Over the last 20+ years, personal branding has become a more common and important topic. Before that, we referred to it as "reputation," but your personal brand is more than just your reputation; it creates emotion in those who are thinking about you.

Back in 2005, I was taking a walk in Center City, Philadelphia with my friend, Brian Fishbone. He is also a corporate trainer and a community builder. He and I met through a group called Company of Friends, a networking group from *Fast Company Magazine.*

As we walked along, we were talking about the importance of honing a personal brand, especially when it comes to career opportunities. He said, "You know, Theresa, your brand is 'love'."

"Really?" I responded. I thought about it. Love is not such a bad brand to have!

In 2013, I was doing a branding exercise with some high school students who were in a program to learn how to create logos and build web pages. It was their "guinea pig" business. They interviewed me to learn about my work so they could create a logo and website for my business.

After much discussion, one astute young woman said, "Theresa, your brand is 'hope.' Your work gives people hope that things will be better. Your work shows people possibilities." Wow. Hope is not a bad brand to have, either.

When did all this personal branding become a thing? In 1996, when Tom Peters published the article, "A Brand Called You" in *Fast Company Magazine.*

In the piece, Peters discusses the need for each of us to see ourselves as an independent company — a company of one — even if a larger company employs us. You see, in the '90s there was a shift toward re-engineering. This shift compressed organizations, created reorganizations, and, as a result, many people were displaced. Many companies were going through a reduction in workforce, which was called "downsizing." Interestingly enough, as the bodies were shed, the salaries and bonuses of executive leaders went up. (That's how we got to this huge divide between the "haves" and the "have much less." But, I digress.)

Since employees no longer had the security of lifetime employment, Peters argued, they had to start thinking like entrepreneurs. As an employee, you were a commodity. Instead, think of yourself as a company of one.

I adopted this thinking, and it has helped me survive and thrive for decades in a changing work environment. As a company of one, you need a good brand.

Think about Tiffany & Co. What words come to mind? Special occasion. Expensive. Luxury, Teal blue box. Engagement.

How about Disney? Fun. Family. Happiest place on earth. Children. Amazing experience.

Now, insert your name. What words come to mind when people think of you? More importantly, what words must come to mind to be respected and have career opportunities?

There's an exercise I love to do with groups so they can informally gather individual branding. I call it the "pat on the back" exercise. You tape a paper plate or piece of white card stock to your back (usually a friend will help you). Then you go around the room, and each person writes one or two words on the paper that remind them of you. At the end of the exercise, you end up with a page of words that represent your brand.

Once I conducted this exercise with some colleagues in Northern Ireland. Upon conclusion of the exercise, one of the young men came up to me on the break and said, "I want you to take a look at my list." There were about 15 comments, and 9 of them were "Quiet."

I said, "Well, it looks like people see you as quiet."

He responded, "I know. But I don't want that to be my brand."

So I asked him, "What might you do to change your brand?"

He laughed and said, "I guess I need to speak up more!"

"Indeed, you will!" I responded.

There's the challenge. First, you need to determine what your brand is: What words come to mind when they think of you? Then, determine for yourself what the brand you want and/or need to have is to achieve your career goals. If your current brand does not align with the brand you need, what might you do?

TO CREATE THE BRAND YOU WANT, YOU MUST CREATE THE EXPERIENCES THAT WILL SUPPORT THAT BRAND.

For me, as a solopreneur, it's crucial that I have the kind of brand that not only gets me hired, but also sustains a solid business relationship. My brand should include some or all of the following:

- Competent
- Easy to work with
- Trustworthy
- Fun
- Problem solver

HOW ABOUT YOU? WHAT IS YOUR CURRENT BRAND?
ASK A FEW TRUSTED COLLEAGUES WHAT WORDS COME TO MIND WHEN THEY THINK OF YOU?

CURRENT BRAND:

IF YOU'D LIKE TO GET MORE FORMAL, THERE ARE A COUPLE TOOLS YOU CAN USE TO DETERMINE YOUR CURRENT BRAND.

JOHARI WINDOW / NOHARI WINDOW

RESULTS:

_____

_____

_____

_____

_____

360 FEEDBACK
a. Formal – There are a number of excellent tools

   i. https://www.getapp.com/p/sem/360-degree-feedback-software

b. Informal – Send an email or do an in-person request. Ask each person 2 questions:

   i. When you think of me, what is it that I do best? What are my strengths?

   ii. If I were to do one thing better or differently, something that might be getting in the way of my success, what would that be?

WHAT IS YOUR IDEAL BRAND, BASED ON YOUR CAREER GOALS?

IDEAL BRAND:

_____

_____

_____

WHAT MIGHT YOU DO AND WHAT EXPERIENCES CAN YOU CREATE THAT WOULD LEAD TO YOUR IDEAL BRAND?

_____

_____

_____

IN ADDITION TO THE EXPERIENCES YOU CREATE, WHAT OTHER FACTORS IMPACT YOUR BRAND?

_____

_____

_____

SEE THE ADDENDUM FOR A CHECKLIST OF THINGS ON LINKEDIN THAT ARE IMPORTANT.

Everything you post, and every post you like or comment on, should tie to your personal brand. Why? Because everything your connections see with your name attached to it will link that content to you.

Unfortunately, LinkedIn has taken on a "Facebook-like" feel over the years. It's not Facebook. LinkedIn is the one social media platform that was intended for professional networking. Do your best to treat it as such. Save your personal posts for Facebook or Instagram.

As for the other social media platforms, you're encouraged to use the same mindset – ensure that everything you post or like aligns with your brand. You may be thinking, "Can't I just relax and have some fun?" Yes, you can — as long as what you post wouldn't hurt you in a job situation. Even if your profile is locked or set to "friends only", people can still take screenshots and pass along your posts and comments. I would err on the side of caution.

SOME FACTORS THAT IMPACT YOUR BRAND INCLUDE:

Appearance:
•Clothing, Hairstyle, Makeup, Nails, Accessories, Shoes

• Education level
• Professional certifications
• Publications
• Places you've worked
• Current and past job titles
• Where you live
• What you drive
• Who's in your professional circle?
• Who's in your social circle?
• What comes up on Google?

Social media presence:
• LinkedIn, Facebook, TikTok, Instagram, "X" (Twitter)
• Others

No matter what platform you use, your presence (or lack thereof) contributes to your brand. LinkedIn is the primary platform for professional networking and conversation. If you're going to have a presence on LinkedIn — and you should — you want to ensure that your profile is solid and what you share is aligned with the brand you want.

I enjoy Facebook for the ability to stay in touch with a geographically dispersed group of family and friends. Everything I post aligns with these rules:

1) Does it inform, entertain, uplift, and/or enlighten? If the post supports any of these, I am inclined to share it.

2) Could the post possibly offend, stir the pot, or tarnish my brand? If it could do any of these, I am inclined not to share it.

I avoid anything political, religious, or any other topic that could potentially create harsh judgment or drama. It's just not worth it. I tend to post quotes, cat / food / vacation pictures, and interesting articles. I advertise a lot of events, including my own and others'. Everything I post aligns with my brand.

WHAT MIGHT YOU DO, OR DO DIFFERENTLY, TO ALIGN YOUR SOCIAL MEDIA ACTIVITY WITH THE PERSONAL BRAND YOU WANT?

IS THERE ANYTHING YOU MIGHT STOP DOING ON SOCIAL MEDIA TO ENSURE THE INTEGRITY OF YOUR PERSONAL BRAND?

WHAT MIGHT YOU INCLUDE IN YOUR SOCIAL MEDIA ROUTINE TO STRENGTHEN YOUR PERSONAL BRAND?

A final thought on personal branding: help others. Be nice. There was a great book about the power of helping others that impacted my thinking: "The Go-Giver: A Little Story About a Powerful Business Idea," by Bob Burg and John D. Mann. It is a story about the power of giving. It teaches the *Five Laws of Stratospheric Success*, each based on how much you provide value, serve, help, give of yourself, and are open to receiving.

I have built my business on the power of giving. Since 2003, I have been helping job seekers at no cost. I speak for and coordinate job search groups. I assist individual job seekers. I introduce job seekers to career coaches I love and trust. Over the years, I have dedicated thousands of hours to this cause with no regrets. Nothing is as noble as helping others understand themselves better, find a job, and build a career.

WHAT ARE WAYS YOU CAN ADD VALUE FOR AND/OR HELP OTHERS?

WHAT ARE ACTS OF SERVICE YOU CAN PROVIDE?

WHAT ARE WAYS YOU CAN GIVE OF YOURSELF?

HOW CAN OTHERS HELP YOU?

"Formal education will make you a living; self-education will make you a fortune."

Jim Rohn

Education

Third-party validation is another critical component of "the sails" of your career boat. Completing levels of education, earning degrees and certifications, and completing courses of study adds to your credibility.

COLLEGE

For many years, and still now to some degree, having a college education became a ticket of admission for many jobs. As time went on and more people attained 4-year degrees, many jobs started to require graduate degrees as well.

In the last decade or so, things started to change. Employers began to realize that there were excellent candidates who had not completed formal education beyond high school. We're starting to see more and more jobs that say, "Bachelor's degree, or equivalent experience." I believe that trend will continue.

Having said that, it's still helpful to have third-party validation. I won't get into a lot of detail here, except to say that you should consider the ROI (return on investment) of any formal education you pursue. There should be a reasonable return on your investment for the amount of time and money you invest.

Here's an example:

Kevin wanted to attain an undergraduate degree in psychology. He applied to and was accepted at a local university with an outstanding reputation. The cost for tuition and fees was $44,440 per year. He took out student loans to cover the cost. By graduation, he owed $177,760.00 + interest. Upon graduation, he realized that there weren't any jobs in his field that didn't require a graduate degree and a license to practice. He took a break, worked at a local convenience store making $12/hour, and was tasked with paying back the sizable loan.

If he did pursue a master's degree at the same school, at $30,770 per year for 3 years, he would add another $92,310 to his debt, resulting in a total debt of $270,070 + interest.

According to the Bureau of Labor and Statistics (BLS), the average annual income for a psychologist is $85,340.

It will take him years to pay off the debt and start to see a return on his investment of time and money.

Beth took a different path. She spent her first two years at a community college at $10,350 a year. Upon completion of her associates degree, she transferred to a state school at $11,058 a year, and majored in information technology. Upon graduation, her school loans totaled $42,816, plus interest. She immediately got a job in IT working with a local company that paid her a starting salary of $45,000. She had full benefits and paid vacation.

Her company offered tuition reimbursement up to $5,250 per year. She enrolled in an online university that cost $4,325 every six months (unlimited credits) to pursue an MBA in information technology management. While working, she completed all of the coursework within 24 months. Her company paid $10,500 toward her tuition, and she covered the other $6,800 herself. No loans were taken.

By the time she was 28, she was promoted to a manager of IT making $90,000 annually.

There are a number of variables to weigh, but, ultimately, it comes down to ROI.

If you:
• Are academically gifted
• Have a family that will pay for your schooling
• Can win a scholarship
• Can get a significant amount of financial aid

By all means, go to the school of your choice.

If you:
• Are average or below academically
• Are from a family that can contribute little to pay for school
• Don't have any scholarships
• Can't get much financial aid

Consider a more reasonably priced education path.

Be smart about your choices. You can get an excellent education with the combo community college + state school deal. And, there are reasonably priced options for both undergraduate and graduate degrees through some reputable online universities, such as Western Governors University.

Another option is to get a job with a company that pays tuition reimbursement and attend school while you're building valuable experience and your professional network. You accrue little to no student debt. When you graduate, you already have a job. You can choose to stay, or move on to another company. Yes, it will take longer to complete the degree. But the tradeoff of little to no school debt and building valuable job experience might be worth it.

CERTIFICATES AND CERTIFICATIONS

Let's talk about certificate and certification programs. I can't say enough good things about them! What I love most is that the training is direct with no fluff. If you pursue a certification, like the PHR (Professional in Human Resources) through HRCI, the coursework is directly related to your field. At the time of publication, the cost of the PHR exam is $395, with an additional $100 application fee. If you choose to participate in a group study program, expect to invest an additional $1,000 to $2,000.

Note: SHRM (Society for Human Resource Management) offers its own certifications – the SHRM-CP and SHRM-SCP – with a similar price range.

The Project Management Institute (PMI) also offers a very reputable certification. As of this writing, the PMP exam costs $555 for non-members and $405 for PMI members. PMI membership is $129/year with a $10 application fee. You'll also want the PMBOK Guide to study – that's $65.95 for non-members and $49.50 for members.

See why I love certifications? They're much more reasonably priced than degree programs, and you can complete them in less time. The tradeoff is that you'll usually need to maintain your designation with continuing education hours each year.

Still, it's a great investment! Even if you already have a graduate degree, adding a certification is a feather in your cap.

LOW-HANGING FRUIT AND LOW-COST

There are many low-priced and even free educational resources online. I love LinkedIn Learning! The courses are well-done and are taught by industry thought leaders and educators. As you complete each course, you can add it directly to your LinkedIn profile. You will need a premium subscription to LinkedIn to have access. But once you do, you can take as many courses as you want.

Other great online resources for free or reasonably priced courses:

• **UDEMY** – Affordable courses on a wide range of professional and personal development topics; often includes lifetime access.

• **COURSERA** – University and industry-led courses; many free to audit with optional certificates. Offers professional certificates and degree programs.

• **EDX** – University-level courses from institutions like Harvard and MIT; free to audit, with certificates available for a fee.

• **FUTURELEARN** – Offers short courses and microcredentials from global universities and institutions; many free with upgrade options.

• **ALISON** – Free online courses in workplace skills, business, technology, and health; certificates and diplomas available for a small fee.

• **SKILLSHARE** – Subscription-based platform focused on creative, business, and tech skills; offers a free trial period.

• **KHAN ACADEMY** – Completely free platform focused on foundational subjects like math, science, economics, and more; no certificates, but excellent content.

• **GOOGLE CAREER CERTIFICATES (VIA COURSERA)** – Affordable, job-ready training in fields like IT support, data analytics, UX design, and project management.

• **MIT OPENCOURSEWARE** – Free access to real MIT course content across a wide range of subjects; no certificates, but world-class education.

• **SAYLOR ACADEMY** – Free college-level courses; optional low-cost exams to earn certificates or even transfer credit.

• **OPENLEARN (BY THE OPEN UNIVERSITY)** – Free courses with digital badges or statements of participation in various topics.

• **HUBSPOT ACADEMY** – Free certifications in inbound marketing, social media, sales, and customer service; well-regarded in digital marketing fields.

MONEY IS NO OBJECT?

If you've got the cash, why not upgrade your education—and your brand—with a certificate from a prestigious institution?

In 2023, I jumped into the deep end with a year-long executive certificate program from Wharton for Chief Human Resource Officers (CHROs). I won't sugarcoat it—it was expensive. The full cost was $20,000, but I locked in early at $18,500. And yes, I paid out of pocket. Ca-ching! It was also time-consuming—I averaged more than 10 hours of work a week, including a live instructor session and a heavy dose of self-study.

It was 100% worth it.

I wrote a capstone project that became the foundation for my SHRM keynote, From Tactical to Transformational: The Path to Exceptional HR." I expanded my network to include senior HR leaders from around the world. And I walked away with insights not only in HR, but in broader business trends that help me speak the language of the C-suite.

In addition to Wharton (University of Pennsylvania), check out other top-tier programs like:

• Harvard Business School
• MIT Sloan School of Management
• Stanford Graduate School of Business
• Kellogg School of Management (Northwestern)
• Columbia Business School
• University of Chicago Booth School of Business

WHAT'S THE COST?

At the time of publication, short executive education programs (typically 3–7 days) from top-tier schools range from $3,000 to $12,000, depending on the topic and institution. Longer programs—like certificate series that span several months to a year—can range from $15,000 to $35,000 or more. Many offer online or hybrid formats to accommodate working professionals. The price tag is significant, but if you choose wisely, the return on investment can be career-changing.

And don't forget to explore whether your employer offers tuition reimbursement or professional development funds. Many companies are willing to contribute if the learning aligns with your role or career path.

SECTION 5:
Building Your Motor:
Cultivating Your Professional Network

IN THIS SECTION, WE'LL COVER WAYS TO BUILD YOUR PROFESSIONAL NETWORK: WHY IT MATTERS, WHO IS IN YOUR NETWORK, AND SOCIAL NETWORKING TOOLS.

KNOW PEOPLE | CREDIBILITY | EXPERIENCE | DIRECTION

WHY THIS MATTERS

"The richest people in the world look for and build networks; everyone else looks for work."

Robert Kiyosaki

Professional Networking

You've probably heard the saying, "It's not what you know, it's who you know."

I had the pleasure of participating in an elite women's leadership development program, Women Unlimited, in New York City. The founder, Jean Otte, would say, "It's not what you know. It's who knows you know."

It's not enough to be effective at what you do. People, the right people, need to know you're effective at what you do.

Today, we are blessed with social media. That is a great way to track your network and ensure people "know what you know." We'll get into that in the next section.

Along your career travels, you will have interactions with colleagues and customers. The experience you provide will shape your brand. That brand will stick with them until your next interaction. That could be 10, 20 or 30 years later.

In high school, I got a job working at Roy Rogers Family Restaurant. It was my first job with a paycheck. I really loved that job! Shortly after being hired, I was asked to serve as the hostess. There were several cool things about being the hostess.

First, I was given a fabulous outfit, including a genuine pair of Dingo boots.

Second, I greeted customers as they came in: "Howdy pardners!"

Third, I took care of the dining room, including the salad and fixins bar. I took great pride in that responsibility. My salad bar was immaculate. The veggies were fresh and full, but not too full. The condiments were full. The napkins were full, but not too full. There were no sloppy spills on my salad bar. It was always wiped clean.

Fourth, I poured coffee refills for the guests in the dining room. How awesome is that? Often, we worked in a little conversation. I befriended several of our regulars. And my coffee pots—boy, did they shine! I would take them in the back and scrub them with a Scotch-BriteTM pad. No stains or tarnish on my coffee pots! Folks on the next shift would always know I was on previously by the pristine state of the dining room and the shiny coffee pots. It was a source of pride.

I worked there for a few years, and then went off to college. Decades later, I reconnected with some of my Roy Rogers colleagues. They still think of me for my clean salad bar, shiny coffee pots and friendly demeanor. That brand stuck!

Don't discount those interactions in high school and college. The memories and the brand you create lasts a lifetime! Those relationships can also last that long, at least from a professional network perspective.

WHERE DO YOU MAKE CONNECTIONS?

Family, friends, work colleagues, customers, professional organizations, church, clubs, sports, hobby groups, at the gym, on public transportation, at the grocery store, at the bar, in restaurants…

As we meet new people, we're often asked, "So, what do you do?" I must admit, this is a very American thing. When I travel to other countries they don't go right to the career question.

How do you answer that question? Does it roll off your tongue? Or do you have to stop and think, "What DO I do?" Do you stumble through a disjointed response? Or do you have something smart and concise prepared?

This is your "elevator statement." It's called that because it's something short that can be delivered if you were having a conversation on an elevator ride. It's less than 30-seconds in length.

> **"Networking is not about just connecting people. It's about connecting people with people, people with ideas, and people with opportunities."**
>
> *Michele Jennae*

My Elevator Statement:

I am the president of High Five Performance, Inc., a company that works with leaders to create workplaces where people want to be. We train managers and leaders, working with them to create an ideal culture where their employees can be engaged and productive. On the weekends, I get paid to make people laugh.

To be honest, people home in on that last line. "What? Tell me more?" I tell them I am a professional comedian and have been doing paid comedy for over two decades. It's not my primary business, but it helps to keep me grounded and sharpens my platform skills. It also adds an amazing group of funny people to my professional network.

That last line is often "the hook." It's what creates interest for the listener. A good elevator statement isn't just about telling people what you do, it's about getting the listener to want to know more.

HOW WOULD YOU DEFINE YOURSELF AND WHAT YOU DO?

_____

_____

_____

WHAT IS YOUR ELEVATOR STATEMENT?

_____

_____

_____

_____

WHAT IS "YOUR HOOK" SO PEOPLE WANT TO HEAR MORE?

_____

_____

"Your network is your net worth."

Porter Gale

WHAT IS PROFESSIONAL NETWORKING?

If you're an introvert, the word "networking" probably makes the hair on the back of your neck stand up. Even some extroverts aren't big fans of networking. I'm here to tell you, it's all about your mindset and knowing how to make the experience easier for you.

First, mindset. It's not about you going into an event with an empty bowl like Oliver Twist, "Please, sir. May I have some more?"

No, no, no. It's about knowing what you can offer to help others. By helping others, you will, in turn, be helped. It's like a boomerang. You put good energy out there…SWOOSH…It always comes back.

I was teaching a professional networking class at Temple University in the early 2000s. I read this definition of networking to the class:

Networking is a lifelong process of meeting people, making contacts, and building mutually beneficial professional relationships. It is about wanting to help people who also want to help you.

I had one lady in the class who crossed her arms, turned her head to the side, and rolled her eyes while letting out a huge sigh. I thought, but didn't say out loud, "Wow. What's going on here?"

I asked her, "What are your thoughts on that definition?"

She replied, "It's not true. It's not true at all. No one wants to help me!"

Her other classmates were wide-eyed, looking at her, then looking at me, wondering how I would respond to that.

"Thank you for sharing that. That is real for you, based on your experience. Can I ask you to try one thing, for the sake of this class. Just give me the benefit of the doubt. Be open to THE POSSIBILITY that it could be true."

"I can do that. But I still don't think that's true."

You see, it's all perspective. If you haven't had good experiences networking, that's real for you. That's why you need to create the good experiences you want to have.

Let's tackle the introvert thing first. I know it's daunting to push yourself out of the house to go to the event. That alone is a huge accomplishment. Your nature is to stay at home, read a book, surf the web—alone. Now you're having to get dressed (What to wear?!) … throw business cards in your pocket, drive somewhere…and be in a room full of strangers for a couple of hours. Oy!

Here are some things you can do to take the sting out of networking:

Arrive at the event early to avoid walking into a crowded room. Find a good table where people are likely to approach you, perhaps near the food or the bar.

Volunteer for a role at the meeting, such as serving at the registration desk, greeting attendees, or selling 50/50 tickets. Having a formal role can sometimes make it more comfortable.

If you can access the attendee list in advance, strategically identify those individuals you want to meet and make a list. Consider what topics you want to discuss. You might even reach out before the meeting with a brief introduction.

If you know someone who's attending and is connected to someone you'd like to meet, reach out to them ahead of time and ask if they would be willing to make an introduction.

NETWORKING SUBTLETIES

When you get in a conversation with someone, watch for cues to see if they're still engaged. If the event is about networking, you don't want to monopolize their time, and you need to make sure they don't monopolize your time. If you feel the conversation should be continued later, or that you can help each other professionally, ask them, "May I have a card? I'd like to stay in touch. Perhaps we could continue the conversation." If they have a card, they will give you one, and they will likely ask, "Do you have a card?" Then you can present them with your card as well. A true business card exchange.

Too often, I see people present their business cards first. "Here, take my card. And please let's follow up."

No, no, no.

Now you've given them an assignment. And you've made an assumption that they want to reach out to you. You should always ask for their card first. Never give them an assignment: "Hey, please send me that article that you mentioned."

No, no, no.

"Social media is not a media. The key is to listen, engage, and build relationships."

David Alston

You get their card first. Then you might say, "If you don't mind, I'd like to follow up with you for that article you mentioned. That sounds very interesting."

And this next move is the worst. Oy. I cringe thinking about it.

Before we go further, let's talk about the card itself. Despite what you may have heard, the business card has not gone out of style. Yes, many people now share a QR code on their phone, or use a tap-enabled digital card like Dot or Popl — and those can be great tools. But whether it's a traditional card or a tech-forward option, the same etiquette still applies: you shouldn't shove your contact info at someone first. Always ask for their information first and let them invite you to share yours.

When you hand someone your card (or your QR code), you're essentially saying, "Here, you do the work to follow up with me." But if you take their information first, you maintain the power to connect thoughtfully — and avoid putting the other person on the spot.

On another note – never distribute your bio or resume at a networking event. Never. If it's a job fair, that's appropriate. I can't think of any other situation where that would be appropriate.

SOCIAL MEDIA TOOLS

In the spring of 2003, LinkedIn launched its first public version. In August of that year, I received my first connection invitation from my friend, David Newman. If I'm honest, I was quite cynical about accepting the request. "What the heck is this? Is this going to create spam? I have no time for this nonsense!" But, I really love my friend David. Out of respect for him, I took the leap. Soon, I began receiving additional connection requests. Then, I was sending connection requests. I strictly connected only to people who I really knew – no strangers. Before long, I had more connections than David. David was like, "Hey, you! What are you doing?!" Like me, he was an avid networker.

A year later, I was quite the LinkedIn devotee. By 2005, I was seen as a local thought leader in LinkedIn. I was invited to speak at professional organizations and universities on the topic. I never received payment for it, but speaking further increased my network.

Little did I know how that simple connection request from David would lead to being a part of a networking revolution. Today, LinkedIn is the premier business networking tool. If you're not on it, hop in! If you are, let's make sure your profile is optimized.

See the Addendum for a nice checklist for your LinkedIn profile. Mind you, the platform is constantly changing and evolving, so you'll need to poke around to find things if they aren't obvious.

A few things that are relatively easy and super important:

Have a LinkedIn profile picture. The picture should capture you with the brand you want. Even if you take a nice photo with your phone, that's good enough.

Not having a picture is a bad idea. I've had people say, "Well, I don't want them to see how old I am," or "I'd rather they not know I'm a person of color." Don't worry about that. They are going to find out soon enough. And do you really want to work for a company that wouldn't hire you because you're older or a person of color? No.

Include a nice banner behind your profile picture. There are many pages and apps (e.g. Canva) that have canned banners, and other pages that will show you how to create your own customized banner. Take the time to do this. It will create the right vibe for your profile and will show that you cared enough to make it look nice.

Include a summary that is concise and interesting to read. It might be like your elevator speech. Something short that paints a clear picture of who you are and what you do.

Some other things that will help you score bonus points on your profile:

If you've been out of school for a while, be sure to include professional development that you've had in the last few years. You want your education to appear fresh and demonstrate that you are keeping up with the latest in your field. This includes any certifications, certificate programs, non-credit or credit coursework completed through colleges or educational vendors, as well as online coursework.

Get some recommendations from trusted colleagues and customers. This will provide another perspective on your strengths and skills. There are two ways to get recommendations.

1. You can reach out to any connected individual and ask them if they would be kind enough to write up and post one for your profile. Many people respond positively to these requests.

2. Another fun way to get a recommendation is to proactively post a recommendation on their page first. Once they accept your recommendation, LinkedIn will ask them, "Would you like to post a recommendation for this person?" Many people respond in kind.

3. Either option will help to beef up your recommendations and your brand.

Follow groups and pages that are related to your field. Often recruiters will scan to see who you are following.

If this seems a bit overwhelming, you can hire someone to optimize your profile for a fee.

What about other social media?

By far, LinkedIn is the first place recruiters will look for you. They might also Google you to find other places where you have a presence. Remember that MySpace page that you never deleted? It's still out there. Facebook and Instagram are other platforms that will be reviewed.

On Facebook, it's smart to set your profile settings to "friends only" so the general public can't see everything you post. I know you're going to cry, "First Amendment! Freedom of Speech," when I tell you that you really shouldn't post everything you think and feel on Facebook. Here are things that may weed you out of the interview pile:

Photos of you or others:

Drinking. You wanted to post that picture of the mongo bloody Mary from that cool restaurant in Vegas. Make sure that is visible to **friends only**. Or better yet, forgo the urge.

Scantily dressed. Unless you're applying for a role that requires that type of attire, let's keep the clothes on.

Political posts:

In the United States, we've become a divided country. As much as you may take pride in your political beliefs, the person reviewing your profile might play for another team. That would be a shame to be plucked out of the interview pile for sharing a political post.

You should consider every post, regardless of your privacy settings. "Is this something I would want a recruiter to see?" If the answer is no, don't post it.

If you haven't already done this, Google yourself. What do you find? Hopefully, it's all good. Here are some things folks can find that might weed you out of the interview pile:

DUIs or other arrests. Most companies will do a background check and find these things whether they are available via a Google search or not. I know a senior VP that has a DUI in her Google search. She was already gainfully employed when she was arrested. Sadly, an employee who was applying for work in her department found the DUI when she did a Google search. The employee was hired, and told others in the company about what she had found online.

Look for filed complaints to groups like the Better Business Bureau, for example. A man I met during my travels seemed like a genuinely nice guy. Yet, when I was doing some research before sending a referral his way, I found a litany of complaints of fraud and rip-off scams from about 10 years ago. Needless to say, I didn't send any referrals his way.

What if you have these types of items in your Google search? You will need a strong explanation to restore your credibility and convince folks that you are a changed person.

FEEDING & MAINTAINING YOUR NETWORK

You have a LinkedIn profile you are proud of. Now it's a matter of keeping your profile and your networking up to date. There are a few schools of thought when it comes to LinkedIn connections:

PURIST: I only connect with people I know and trust.

80/20: 80% of my network are people I know and trust. 20% are people I've met in my online or in-person travels, and I believe we can help one another.

LION (LINKEDIN NETWORKER): I connect with EVERYONE.

One style is not any better than the other; it's a matter of why you want connections. Folks in sales-related roles typically want to be connected to as many people as possible. Being a LION might make sense for them.

People who have their own business, or are in roles where collaboration with other professionals is beneficial, might benefit more from an 80/20 LinkedIn network.

"All things being equal—people will do business with and refer business to those people they know, like and trust."

Bob Burg and John David Mann,
The Go-Giver

Those who work for another company and only search for jobs every now and then might benefit from a Purist LinkedIn network.

My rule of thumb is to subscribe to the 80/20 rule. As I attend events and meet people along my travels, I ask myself, "Is it possible that I could be helpful to this person, or they could be helpful to me?" If the answer is yes, I usually ask for their business card and reach out with a LinkedIn invitation to connect. I always send a short note, "I enjoyed our conversation at the XYZ event last night. If you think it would be mutually beneficial, let's connect and stay in touch."

As I receive connection requests from strangers, I ask "Is it possible that I could be helpful to this person, or they could be helpful to me?" If the answer is yes, I might accept their request. If the answer is no, or I still have some doubts, I send a LinkedIn message to them, "Thanks for reaching out. Forgive me, but I've forgotten where we met. Thanks in advance for refreshing my memory!"

It's important to consider, "Who do I want in my network?" Depending on your career objectives, you'll want to target specific kinds of people strategically. For example, if you're a clinical project manager in a pharmaceutical company, and plan to stay in that field, you'll want to connect with any colleagues who have a sense of your skills and work product, or those who do similar work at other companies. (Pharma friends, what I've noticed over time is that people tend to hop around. Over time, you'll see a colleague go from Merck, to Sanofi, to J&J, to AstraZeneca, to Bayer. That's helpful to you if you're shopping around for a new job in that industry. Follow and feed those connections!)

If you are in sales, you will want to connect to people who buy your product or service or can recommend you to someone who does. If you sell an LMS (Learning Management System), for example, you'll want to connect with training, human resources, and organizational development professionals. What you sell will also dictate where you do a lot of your professional networking.

PRUNING YOUR NETWORK
I would say at least once a year, you should review your LinkedIn connections and remove those with whom you've had little contact, and/or you doubt there is any mutual benefit to being connected. I also weed out those that have a "bad brand." I don't want to be associated with folks who have a tarnished brand.

FEEDING YOUR NETWORK
Now that you know how to build your network and track it on LinkedIn, it's time to learn how to keep it fresh and vibrant. You want to stay top-of-mind.

One of the most critical and often overlooked things is the "follow-up." When you meet someone at a networking event that could lead to a valuable relationship, be sure to follow up with a short note. If they mentioned they are taking a big trip, going to see their new grandchild, or are presenting at a major conference, for example, follow up with a nice note to ask how it went. They will be pleasantly surprised to see that you cared enough to remember and ask.

It's also a good idea to scan your LinkedIn news feed once a day. "Like" or comment on those posts that resonate with your brand. Each "like" or comment sends the post to your connections' news feeds. The goal here is to stay top of mind.

If you're particularly energetic, you can create your own posts and include memes, articles or your own thoughts on a topic. If you're a thought leader in your field, you might want to write your own articles. They become part of your profile, and folks can click on your articles to read up on your thoughts and ideas. Assuming you're a decent writer, that is a real credibility builder.

SECTION 6:
Sailing to Chosen Destinations:
Finding Work

TOOLS OF THE TRADE
- **RESUME**
- **LINKEDIN PROFILE**
- **ONE-PAGER**
- **TARGET COMPANIES LIST**
- **INFORMATIONAL INTERVIEWS**

WHY THIS MATTERS

"In a world of noise, clarity is power. Your job search materials should make people think, 'I know exactly why we need them.'"

Theresa Hummel-Krallinger

Resumes

Several tools are helpful in a job search. The most universal tool is the resume. Depending on the job you want and the industry, you will need a solid resume or a CV (Curriculum Vitae). Either way, it's a document that gives a snapshot of who you are, where you've been, your skills and knowledge, and what value you can add.

Today's job seekers are blessed, as most of us can easily pull together a simple resume ourselves using Microsoft Word. There are two kinds of resumes: chronological and functional. The most common is the chronological resume, which emphasizes work experience, in reverse chronological order, listing the most recent job first. The functional resume emphasizes skills and talents you have developed and de-emphasizes job titles, employers' names, and dates.

Indeed.com had some great samples and information for each:

Here's a great explanation of a chronological resume with a video: https://www.indeed.com/career-advice/resumes-cover-letters/chronological-resume-tips-and-examples

Here's info on a functional resume: https://www.indeed.com/career-advice/resumes-cover-letters/functional-resume-tips-and-examples

And the Curriculum Vitae (CV): https://www.indeed.com/career-advice/resumes-cover-letters/cv-format-guide

If you want to ensure your resume is in great shape, have a professional do it for you. There's a great professional organization where you can find a career counselor: NCDA (National Career Development Association.) You can do a search using your zip code / postal code to find one near you. These individuals can either create your resume for you or refer you to someone credible who can.

https://ncda.org/aws/NCDA/pt/sp/consumer_find

Another option that is reasonably priced is www.Fiverr.com. There are folks that will happily do your resume for anything from $15 to $200.

LinkedIn Profile

We talked about this in previous chapters. I can't emphasize enough the importance of having a complete profile. See the LinkedIn Checklist in the Addendum.

One-Pager

If you're a solo practitioner or owner of a small company, the one-pager is the job search tool for you. It is a marketing sheet used to promote your company or "company of one." It's not a resume, though it does have some resume components. It should answer the questions:

> "Who are you?"
> "What do you do?"
> "How can I contact you?"

There's a sample one-pager in the Addendum.

Informational Interviews

An informational interview is a great way to build your network and get information about a career choice, a specific job, or a particular company. The best way to get an informational interview is through a virtual introduction from a friend or colleague. You can also reach out directly to people you don't know with your request. The purpose of this conversation is not for the person to connect you with a job opening. The purpose is to gather their opinion on your field, a job opening at their company, or getting information about the company itself.

As the conversation progresses, you might be able to get into more specific job information. The interview should last approximately 15 minutes, and definitely not more than 30 minutes.

Before asking others for help, it's a good idea to have the following items completed and ready to share, as appropriate. The more specific you can be about what you want, the better the information you'll get.

- Quick intro ("elevator speech")
- Resume or one-pager
- Business card (if meeting in person)
- Optimized LinkedIn profile
- Target job titles
- Target company list
- Top marketable skills/strengths
- Accomplishment stories
- Differentiators (Why should people hire you?)

• Salary range
• Geographic area you're willing to travel for work
• How you're currently making use of your professional network
• What other job search networking you're doing
• How you're using social media for your job search
• What online sites/tools you're using for job search
• And a list of questions you have for the person you're meeting with

That might seem like a long list, because it is! But that's the foundation of your job search. You will have done the legwork in defining your job search goal and requirements, which will make it easier for folks to give advice and point you in the right direction.

Once you have those things in place, then it's all about working your network and building your brand online and in person.

Places to Work
Corporate Culture

Whenever I speak with job seekers, they ask, "Where are the good places to work? How do I find them?" These smart job seekers know they're not just looking for work or a job: they want a place that's a good fit.

In the first chapter, we talked about the number of hours we spend working. It's a lot. That's why it's so important we find not only the right kind of work for ourselves, but also a workplace with a healthy culture.

How do you determine if a workplace has a healthy culture?

1. Talk to someone who works there. If you don't know someone personally, use LinkedIn to search for current employees.

2. Look at their website. Read their mission, vision, and values. Look at their careers page.

3. If you get an interview there, how are you treated at reception? What is the reception area like?

4. Is this company on a Best Places to Work or Great Places to Work list?

5. Go to Glassdoor and see what employees are saying about them. Check out other sites like Vault and LinkedIn.

6. When you talk to HR, the hiring manager, or another employee there, ask them these questions:

   a. What behaviors are rewarded here? The people who are getting promoted and getting good raises/bonuses, what are they doing?

   b. What behaviors are criticized here?

   c. What behaviors are modeled by your leaders here?

   d. What is a compelling reason to work here?

Target Companies List

One of the most helpful tools of the trade is one that many job seekers miss: the target companies list. This is where you'll identify the companies you'd like to work for. Job seekers often ask, "Where do I find these companies?" and "How many companies should be on my list?" The answer is, "It depends."

To find target companies, I usually start on LinkedIn. Once I've identified the job title(s) I'm looking for, I consider what companies have that job title. For example, let's say I'm looking for a "Training Specialist" job. We'll start with companies that I know hire trainers. From there, I consider other companies that are likely to have a training department or at least a training position available. Folks that work in support functions, like training, will have a larger selection of companies.

What if you're looking for a job as a biostatistician. You'll be looking, primarily in the pharmaceutical or healthcare fields. I would start with the companies you know – let's say, Merck. Find their company page on LinkedIn. If you scroll down on the right, you'll see a list of "Pages people also viewed." You might see Pfizer, GSK and Novartis. Just below them, you'll see "See all similar pages." Now you'll see Bayer, Roche, AstraZeneca, Abbott, Boehringer Ingelheim. As you click on the different companies, you'll see one or two new ones on the list. Start using this to build your target companies list.

How many companies should you list? It depends on the type of job and the market. I usually recommend people shoot for 25 companies.

You'll see a sample Target Company List in the Addendum.

When you do informational interviews and are networking, it's helpful to have this list handy so you can ask the folks you are meeting with:

1. What do you know about these organizations?

2. Are there any companies not on my list that I should consider?

3. Who do you know at these target companies? Would you be willing to make an introduction?

With each informational interview, you will strengthen your list of target companies and the people you can reach out to within them.

TARGET COMPANY LIST TRACKING TEMPLATE

Company Name / Website / City	People / Contacts	Application Date / Resume Sent	Follow-up Date

SECTION 7:
Passport for Continuous Sailing:
Lifelong Job Insurance

- **MOMENTUM: GETTING IT, MAINTAINING IT**
- **SHARPENING THE SAW**
- **YOUR PERSONAL BOARD OF DIRECTORS**

WHY THIS MATTERS
"Momentum begets momentum, and the best way to start is to start."

Gil Penchina

Momentum

At the start of this book, I discussed setting yourself up so you're always employable. Looking back at what I have done for over 20 years and what others who are always employable do, here's a list of behaviors that will help you build momentum:

1. Love yourself
2. Help others
3. Be really good at something, or several things
4. Make sure other people know you're good at something
5. Keep your resume up to date
6. Keep your LinkedIn profile up to date
7. Give and request LinkedIn recommendations and endorsements
8. Make good use of social media
9. Get active in at least one professional organization
10. Build a strong personal brand
11. Embrace lifelong learning
12. Obtain and maintain solid credentials and third-party validation: degrees, certifications, licenses
13. Build and maintain a strong professional network
14. Go to at least one networking event each month (in person or online)
15. Be an advocate for job seekers
16. Take care of your mental and physical health
17. When asking folks for help, also ask them, "What can I do to help you?"
18. Follow up with folks you meet on your travels
19. Do what you say you'll do
20. Live within your means
21. Have enough saved to cover your bills for 6 months
22. Prepare an annual professional development plan that includes improving a skill or building a new one each year
23. Write and publish blog entries, articles, or LinkedIn articles / posts
24. Speak!
25. Take a personal retreat once a year with time for reflection and to build self-awareness
26. Have a personal mission and values and live according to them
27. Be present
28. Connect people who should know each other
29. Read your city's Business Journal and know what's going on locally
30. Know the market value for your job and the job outlook for your field
31. Read and follow the thought leaders in your field

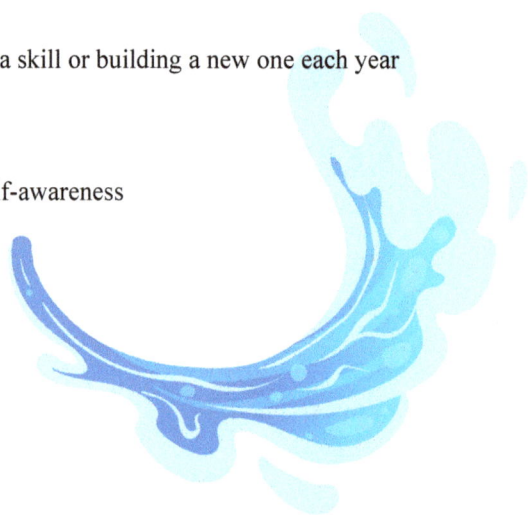

THE MORE OF THESE THINGS YOU DO, THE MORE MOMENTUM YOU'LL HAVE.

HOW MANY ITEMS CAN YOU CHECK OFF?

_____

_____

_____

WHAT ITEMS DO YOU MOST NEED TO FOCUS ON?

_____

_____

_____

ARE THERE ITEMS THAT AREN'T ON THE LIST AND SHOULD BE THERE FOR YOU?

_____

_____

_____

Sharpening the Saw

In the classic, "7 Habits of Highly Effective People," author Stephen Covey has an entire chapter on "Sharpening the Saw." Effective people ensure that they continuously learn and grow. It's easy to become complacent. You completed your formal education. You have a job. So you get into your daily routine and watch the calendar pages fly by. Before you know it, it's been 5 years or more, and you may not have done anything to freshen your skills and knowledge.

When I was working in a pharma company, there was a man in his 40s who had been with the organization for over 12 years. In that time, he didn't join or participate in a professional organization. He didn't attain any new certifications or degrees. The only classes he took were the ones offered by his company. He hadn't dusted off his resume or kept up his LinkedIn profile. He hadn't worked to beef up his professional network beyond the colleagues and clients that he interacted with day to day. He was making a nice salary and bonus each year, so he bought a really nice home in an affluent area. He had a car payment, big mortgage, high local taxes, and two children that were getting ready to go to college.

He and I had a conversation one day. He could feel what was happening. He didn't love his job and hadn't kept himself sharp in the field or in the good graces of the influencers in the organization. I encouraged him to either make a career change that aligned with his interests or embrace his situation and do everything he could to make himself more relevant and valuable. He agreed. And then, did nothing.

A few years later, the organization was not hitting its financial targets. They had to trim headcount. Sadly, he was let go.

He had tremendous debt and financial obligations and a skill set that was not commensurate with the jobs that would provide an income he needed to cover it. It was super stressful for him and his family.

I wish I could say this is uncommon. It's not. Over the years, I have seen many of my colleagues spend up to and beyond their means and not prepare themselves to make a jump to another job.

I share this story to emphasize the importance of sharpening your saw. Staying sharp includes having the latest skills and knowledge in your field. It's staying connected to thought leaders and others in your field. It's having a sense of which organizations might be another place you might like to work. It's also making sure— if you want to stay at your current organization—that your brand is strong with its influencers, the people who make the key decisions or influence those that do.

I hear you saying, "I just want to go to work and do my job. Do I really have to do all of this?"

Do you have to? No. It all depends on the outcome you want. Do you want job insurance? If so, you'll have to pay for it with effort.

12 MONTHS FROM NOW, WHAT ARE SOME THINGS YOU'D LIKE TO BE BETTER AT?

HOW WILL YOU ACCOMPLISH THOSE DEVELOPMENT GOALS?

Your Personal Board of Directors

No successful person ever got there alone. Even the very successful Bill Gates was mentored by Warren Buffett.

In Jim Collins' classic book, "Good to Great," he talks about having a personal board of directors. These are folks you can count on for advice and information to help you succeed and the kick in the pants you might need to stay on track.

You select your personal board of directors. I must say, my husband, Rik, is on my board of directors. He might even be chairman of the board! While he is not in the same field, he is aware of my goals and aspirations. He'll follow along as I make choices and ask, "Is that the best use of your time? Is that in alignment with your goals?"

I also have peers who are striving for similar goals. They're entrepreneurs or solopreneurs who are working to create a successful and sustainable business.

My board also includes others who have achieved things I want to accomplish like meeting financial goals, getting published, and delivering a TedTalk. They can share their experience and shine a light on the path to those accomplishments.

Each year, look at your personal board of directors and assess if you have the right people. Should others be recruited? Should some be retired from your board?

"The quality of our relationships is what determines the quality of our lives."

Esther Perel

WHO'S ON YOUR PERSONAL BOARD OF DIRECTORS?

_____   _____

_____   _____

_____   _____

_____   _____

WHO NEEDS TO BE?

_____   _____

_____   _____

_____   _____

_____   _____

IS THERE ANYONE ON YOUR BOARD OF DIRECTORS THAT HAS OUTLIVED THEIR USEFULNESS AND NEEDS TO BE RETIRED FROM YOUR BOARD?

_____

_____

_____

_____

_____

_____

_____

_____

DO YOU SERVE ON ANYONE ELSE'S BOARD OF DIRECTORS? IF SO, WHO? HOW DO YOU ADD VALUE FOR THEM?

_____

_____

_____

_____

_____

_____

SECTION 8:

Make it Happen

> *"My career has been a journey of learning, growing, falling, and rising again. And I wouldn't change a thing."*
>
> Oprah Winfrey

There's a lot to take in if you've read all the advice, tips, and tricks in this book. But even if you only use some of what was shared, you will be well on your way. What are some things you can implement?

TODAY

_____ _____

_____ _____

THIS MONTH

_____ _____

_____ _____

WITHIN THE NEXT 6 MONTHS

_____ _____

_____ _____

THIS YEAR

_____ _____

_____ _____

"The best way to predict the future is to create it."

Peter Drucker

Conclusion

I hope the stories and tools I've shared inspire you to get your boat ready for whatever comes your way, whether the waters are choppy or smooth. Being flexible and open-minded will keep you in the game, wherever you are in your journey.

My other hope for you is that you feel more empowered to chart your own course. Sometimes it takes longer to find your footing in your career. Keep in mind that there's never been another you in the world before. You have unique talents to share in the workplace and beyond.

Yes, it's an increasingly competitive world. Yes, it can feel overwhelming and uncomfortable to put yourself out there. But, you also have a chance to grow your career in exciting ways that feel authentic to you.

Take your time. Consult this book whenever you're feeling lost. And, share this book as a resource to anyone in your life who is struggling to fit in to our modern workplace.

Lastly, lift others up. Be a reliable helper, within reason. Encouragement and support can mean everything to a colleague. Not only will you enjoy better relationships at work, but these people will be more willing to champion you when you rack up career wins.

I would love to hear your stories of what has worked for you from this book and what needs to be in the next edition! Drop me a line at theresa@highfiveperformance.com and let me know.

Appendices

Links included in the appendices were all working at the time of publication.
After publication, links may change, so I'll be updating these lists and links here:

HTTPS://WWW.MEETTHEAUTHORPC.COM/JOBSEEKER.HTML

Appendix A
Career Planning and Self-Awareness Assessments
Free (or reasonably priced)

MYERS BRIGGS (PERSONALITY):
A. https://www.16personalities.com/free-personality-test
B. http://similarminds.com/jung.html

INTERESTS:
C. http://www.mynextmove.org/explore/ip
   *(O*Net Online – also gives market outlook, salaries, and education requirements)*
D. https://www.123test.com/career-test/ *(career aptitude)*

DISC (BEHAVIOR STYLE):
E. https://www.tonyrobbins.com/disc/
F. https://discpersonalitytesting.com/free-disc-test/
G. https://www.123test.com/disc-personality-test/
H. http://www.proception2.com/questionnaire
   ($$ write to theresa@highfiveperformance.com for access codes for 15+ page report)

VALUES:
I. https://www.meettheauthorpc.com/uploads/1/2/1/3/121321324/values_exercise_2021.pdf
J. http://www.valuescentre.com/pva/

Appendix A
Career Planning and Self-Awareness Assessments
Free (or reasonably priced)

STRENGTHS:
K. https://high5test.com/
L. https://www.gallupstrengthscenter.com/home/en-us/strengthsfinder *($$)*
M. http://www.friendlypress.com/ *($)*

EMOTIONAL INTELLIGENCE:
N. https://www.psychologytoday.com/us/test/3203
O. https://www.mindtools.com/pages/article/ei-quiz.htm
P. https://www.ihhp.com/free-eq-quiz/

JOHARI WINDOW:
Q. http://kevan.org/johari

LEARNING STYLES:
R. http://www.educationplanner.org/students/self-assessments/learning-styles.shtml
S. https://www.learning-styles-online.com/inventory/questions.php?cookieset=y

Appendix A
Career Planning and Self-Awareness Assessments
Free (or reasonably priced)

THE BIG FIVE (PERSONALITY):
T. https://www.truity.com/test/big-five-personality-test
U. https://www.understandmyself.com/personality-assessment *($)*

ENNEAGRAM:
V. https://www.enneagraminstitute.com/rheti *($)*

LEFT BRAIN / RIGHT BRAIN:
W. https://www.arealme.com/left-right-brain/en/

GROWTH MINDSET:
X. https://wabisabilearning.com/blogs/mindfulness-wellbeing/growth-mindset-quiz

Appendix B
LinkedIn Checklist

☐ Profile (overall)

☐ Profile Picture

☐ Background Picture

☐ Headline

☐ Customized URL

☐ Contact Info

☐ About (Summary)

☐ Experience

☐ Education

☐ Licenses & Certifications

☐ Skills & Endorsements

☐ Recommendations

☐ Accomplishments (Honors & Awards)

☐ Volunteer Experience

☐ Interests (Following Companies, Influencers, Schools)

☐ Connections

☐ Status Updates

☐ Articles (like Blog Entries)

☐ Liking others' posts

☐ Commenting on others' posts

☐ Reposting others' posts

☐ Groups – join / start one

☐ Groups – post

☐ Groups – ask/answer questions

☐ Messages – stay in touch!

Appendix C
How well are you prepared for your job search?

RATE YOURSELF:

5: Excellent / Role model
4: Very good / Above average
3: Good / Solid
2: Fair / Needs some improvement
1: Not good / Significant work needed

_____ Your mindset and commitment to job search

_____ Self-awareness (personality, values, interests, etc.)

_____ Clarity around target job / companies

_____ Target company list

_____ Target compensation range

_____ Up-to-date skills / knowledge / experience

_____ Appropriate credentials for target job(s)

_____ Professional relationships / professional network

_____ Regularly scheduled networking opportunities

_____ Personal brand

_____ Career documentation: e.g. resume, CV, bio

_____ Accomplishment stories

_____ Elevator speech

_____ Business cards

_____ Letters of recommendation, references

_____ Personal presentation

_____ Interview skills

_____ Social media presence

_____ LinkedIn profile

_____ Use of LinkedIn for job search

_____ Awareness of market outlook for target job(s)

_____ Clarity around personal preferences (travel/ move/commute, financial, etc.)

Appendix D
Sample One Pager

HIGH FIVE PERFORMANCE, INC.

Theresa Hummel-Krallinger

Theresa Hummel-Krallinger is an international speaker, performance consultant, and executive coach. Known as the "Corporate Prophet", she is recognized for improving business results through developing effective leaders and creating strong employee engagement.

Areas of Focus

Employee Engagement
Implementing a multi-faceted approach to help create a work environment where employees are inspired and productive – a place where people want to work

Organizational Culture
Identifying and driving the behaviors that will achieve organizational goals, and eliminating behaviors that preclude success.

Technical Managers
Specialized in working with highly analytic, quality-focused, technical and scientific managers on how to increase their emotional intelligence and people management skills

Leadership Development
Self-assessment, coaching and training, that leads to authentic, effective leadership.

Improving Communications
Tools and techniques to help individuals build awareness of their own style, and how to communicate with others to get optimal results.

Career Management
Tools and assessments to help individuals find their best career fit and create a plan for continuous professional development

Customer Sample

Prudential Bristol Myers Squibb Johnson&Johnson FAMILY OF COMPANIES TEMPLE UNIVERSITY SHRM SOCIETY FOR HUMAN RESOURCE MANAGEMENT billtrust

Contact

www.highfiveperformance.com   Theresa@highfiveperformance.com

Appendix E
Sample Target Company List

Your Name

123 Market Street, Philadelphia, PA 19000 | (Your Number) | (Your Email)

Target Company List

Strategy & Management Consulting
• McKinsey & Company
• Boston Consulting Group (BCG)
• Bain & Company
• Protiviti
• ZS Associates
• Kearney

Engineering & Infrastructure Consulting
• Kimley-Horn and Associates, Inc.

Healthcare

• Penn Medicine / Hospital of the University of Pennsylvania
• Children's Hospital of Philadelphia (CHOP)
• Jefferson Health
• Temple Health
• Main Line Health

Nonprofit & Philanthropy
• Feeding America
• United Way Worldwide
• Direct Relief
• The Nature Conservancy
• Salvation Army
• St. Jude Children's Research Hospital

Social Responsibility Leaders (Companies That Care)
• Adobe
• Target
• Hyatt
• Sheetz

Appendix F
Resources to Research Companies

GLASSDOOR
Employee reviews, salaries, and interview experiences.
https://www.glassdoor.com

LINKEDIN
Company pages, employee profiles, and networking insights.
https://www.linkedin.com

COMPARABLY
Workplace culture, leadership, diversity, and compensation ratings.
https://www.comparably.com

VAULT (FIRSTHAND)
Insider company reviews and rankings (especially law, finance, consulting).
https://www.vault.com/company-ratings-research

INDEED
Job postings plus company reviews and salaries.
https://www.indeed.com

HOOVER'S (DUN & BRADSTREET)
Detailed company data and financials (subscription; often free at libraries).
https://www.dnb.com

BUZZFILE
Company listings by industry and geography; useful for niche and small businesses.
https://www.buzzfile.com

CRUNCHBASE
Startup and high-growth company profiles, funding rounds, and investor data.
https://www.crunchbase.com

OWLER
Competitor analysis, company news, and alerts.
https://www.owler.com

CAREERBLISS
Company "happiness scores," salary insights, and employee reviews.
https://www.careerbliss.com

FAIRYGODBOSS
Company ratings and resources focused on women in the workplace.
https://fairygodboss.com

THE MUSE
Company profiles with culture descriptions, photos, and videos.
https://www.themuse.com/companies

BUILT IN
Tech and startup company profiles, salaries, and culture insights.
https://builtin.com/companies

PAYSCALE
Salary benchmarks and compensation research.
https://www.payscale.com

LEVELS.FYI
Detailed pay ranges and career ladders in tech.
https://www.levels.fyi

SALARY.COM
Pay and benefits benchmarking across industries.
https://www.salary.com

BETTER BUSINESS BUREAU (BBB)
Ratings, reviews, and complaint histories, especially for smaller/local firms.
https://www.bbb.org

SEC EDGAR DATABASE
Financials, risk factors, and disclosures for U.S. public companies.
https://www.sec.gov/edgar.shtml

ZIPPIA
Career outcomes, company data, and workforce statistics.
https://www.zippia.com

HANDSHAKE
Employer ratings and opportunities, geared toward students and recent grads.
https://joinhandshake.com

Appendix G
Best Places to Work (US)

SOURCE / LIST	FOCUS / NOTABLE FEATURES
GREAT PLACE TO WORK / FORTUNE 100 (2025)	LARGEST, CERTIFIED WORKPLACES; EMPLOYEE FEEDBACK
GLASSDOOR EMPLOYEES' CHOICE (2025)	TOP LARGE EMPLOYERS BY EMPLOYEE REVIEWS
LINKEDIN TOP COMPANIES	CAREER GROWTH & OPPORTUNITY-BASED RANKINGS
INDEED TOP-RATED WORKPLACES (2025)	EMPLOYEE-RATED WORKPLACES ACROSS INDUSTRIES
COMPARABLY (2025, MULTIPLE AWARDS)	CAREER GROWTH, OUTLOOK, DIVERSITY, LEADERSHIP
PEOPLE'S "100 COMPANIES THAT CARE" (2025)	COMPANIES FOCUSING ON CARE, COMMUNITY, WELL-BEING
USA TODAY TOP WORKPLACES 2025	BROAD INDUSTRY RECOGNITION ACROSS U.S. FIRMS
BUILT IN BEST PLACES TO WORK 2025 (TECH/ STARTUPS)	TECH/STARTUP-SPECIFIC LIST BASED ON DATA METRICS
NICHE "BEST PLACES TO WORK" OR "YOUNG PROFESSIONALS"	COMMUNITY RANKING FOCUS (OPTIONAL, CLARIFY TOPIC)

Appendix H
Pre-work for Informational Interviews and Networking Conversations

Before asking others for help, it's a good idea to have the following items completed and ready to share, as appropriate. The more specific you can be about what you want, the better the information you'll get.

- Quick intro ("elevator speech")
- Resume or one-pager
- Business card
- Optimized LinkedIn profile
- Target job titles
- Target company list
- Top marketable skills / strengths
- Accomplishment stories
- Differentiators (Why should people hire you?)
- Salary range
- Geographic area you're willing to travel for work
- How you're currently making use of your professional network
- What other job search networking you're doing
- How you're using social media for your job search
- What online sites/tools you're using for job search
- And a list of questions you have for the person you're meeting with

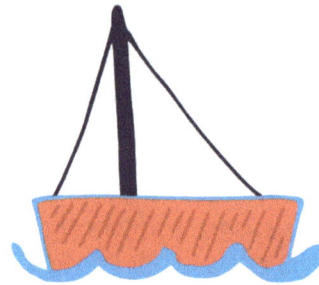

That might seem like a long list, because it is! But that's the foundation of your job search. You will have done the legwork in defining your job search goal and requirements, which will make it easier for folks to give advice and point you in the right direction. Once you have those things in place, then it's all about working your network and building your brand, online and in person.

Acknowledgments

"It takes a village."

This book could never have come to life without the generosity, encouragement, and talents of so many wonderful people.

First, my heartfelt thanks to **Rik Krallinger**, **Dorothy Laincz**, **Trish McShea**, and **Anna Goldfarb** for lending your keen eyes and sharp minds in editing. Your thoughtful feedback and careful attention made the words clearer, stronger, and truer to their intent.

Special gratitude to **Trish McShea** and **Ken Sher**, who gave me the nudges (sometimes gentle, sometimes not so gentle!) I needed to keep going and finally bring this project across the finish line.

To **Hedy Sirico**—thank you for working your layout magic and giving this book the polished, beautiful look it deserves. You made the pages come alive.

Thanks, also, to my assistant, **Darbie Buford**, for getting the book "layout ready."

And to my cruise buddy, **Lou Asner**, thank you for sharing your comics and sprinkling humor throughout these pages. Your wit added lightness and laughter in just the right places.

Each of you played a vital role in shaping this book, and I am deeply grateful.

Notes

Notes

Notes

Notes

_____

_____

_____

_____

_____

_____

_____

_____

_____

_____

_____

_____

Notes

Notes

Notes

Notes

Notes

Notes

_____

_____

_____

_____

_____

_____

_____

_____

_____

_____

_____

_____

About The Author

Theresa Hummel-Krallinger is an Emmy Award-winning speaker, humorist, and professional comedian known for her dynamic, interactive presentations that leave audiences laughing and inspired. A highly respected senior HR and training professional, Theresa has spent over 30 years helping organizations strengthen leadership, enhance culture, and build better workplaces.

Drawing on executive leadership roles in both the financial services and pharmaceutical industries, she combines practical business savvy with an infectious sense of humor. Her ability to help organizations create meaningful performance and engagement strategies has earned her a reputation as a trusted advisor and sought-after speaker on topics such as leadership, career development, organizational culture, and workplace communication.

A lifelong learner and passionate mentor, Theresa is a graduate of the prestigious Women Unlimited leadership program in New York City and Wharton's Executive CHRO program (2023), where she deepened her expertise in strategic HR leadership. She holds certifications in Human Resource Management, Behavior Styles training and coaching, Instructional Design, Adult Learning, and Technical Writing — equipping her with a rich toolbox to support both individuals and organizations.

Theresa is a Past President of the Greater Philadelphia Chapter of the Association for Talent Development (ATD) and a former Toastmasters club president. For 17 years, she shared her expertise as non-credit faculty at Temple University. She has delivered keynote presentations and workshops at regional and international conferences for ATD, SHRM, DIA, the Training Directors Forum, and more.

In addition to her corporate work, Theresa founded and facilitates "Meet the Author at the Pyramid Club," a program recognized as one of Philadelphia's top networking associations by the *Philadelphia Business Journal* 11 years running. She is also a two-time Emmy winner (2019 and 2021) for her work on the PBS talk show *Counter Culture*.

Above all, Theresa is known for her signature blend of warmth, humor, and heart — helping people find joy and purpose at work and beyond.

Lou Asner has published his work as a cartoonist for over 50 years. He has published cartoons in various magazines and articles on humor in trade journals. His studio is crowded with drawing materials and stacks of books, including magazines of his cartoons gathered over the years, and many of his unpublished cartoons. Lou is a man of word plays and puns, also penning the captions for his cartoons. He uses his wife, children and grandchildren for inspiration. He enjoyed designing cartoons for this book.

www.ingramcontent.com/pod-product-compliance
Lightning Source LLC
Chambersburg PA
CBHW052344210326
41597CB00037B/6250